CW01082924

Original title:
Glimmers of the Unknown

Author: Jasper Montgomery
ISBN HARDBACK: 978-9916-90-644-6
ISBN PAPERBACK: 978-9916-90-645-3

A Symphony of the Unmarked

In shadows deep, the silence sings,
A tune forgotten, lost in springs.
Footsteps echo on hidden trails,
Where mystery weaves its ancient tales.

Veils of twilight cloak the night,
While stars awaken, bringing light.
Each breath a note in nature's song,
Together we dance where we belong.

Whispers Carried by the Wind

The breeze speaks softly through the trees,
In melodies that drift with ease.
Secrets told in rustling leaves,
A dialogue the heart believes.

Carried far on feathered wings,
Across the sky, the essence clings.
Messages from worlds unseen,
In every gust, a whispered dream.

Dawn of the Unknown

Upon the horizon, colors blend,
A canvas where shadows mend.
New beginnings, the sun will rise,
Awakening hopes beneath the skies.

The path ahead is yet unchaste,
Each step a leap into the waste.
Fear may lurk in hidden guise,
But courage lives within the ties.

A Flicker Beneath the Surface

Beneath the calm, a fire glows,
A quiet spark that gently grows.
In depths where silence weaves its thread,
A heartbeat echoes, softly spread.

With every wave, desires swell,
In whispered tides, the secrets dwell.
A world unseen, yet ever near,
In shadows cast, the light is clear.

Serendipity in the Silence

In quiet moments, dreams can bloom,
Soft whispers carry through the gloom.
A gentle touch, a fleeting glance,
In silence, we find our dance.

The world retreats, a sacred space,
In stillness, we embrace our grace.
A spark ignites, a hidden fire,
In silence, we rise, we inspire.

Whispers of the Abyss

Deep beneath the ocean's sway,
Echoes guide the lost, the stray.
Through shadows dark and waters cold,
Whispers tell of stories old.

The abyss sings a haunting tune,
Beneath the stars, beneath the moon.
Secrets swirl like currents near,
In whispers, darkness holds us dear.

Echoes from Beyond

From distant lands, soft echoes call,
Reminders that we are not small.
Stories travel through time and space,
In echoes, we find our place.

Voices woven in the air,
Carrying memories rich and rare.
Each note a thread, a timeless song,
In echoes, we all belong.

Shadows of Hidden Light

In the shadows, secrets hide,
Flickers of truth, like waves of tide.
Beneath the dark, there's always grace,
In hidden light, we find our place.

Silent moments, gently glow,
Where shadows dance, where dreams flow.
Through veils of night, we seek the bright,
In shadows, we embrace the light.

The Alluring Abyss

In shadows deep, where silence dwells,
A siren's call, a tale it tells.
The depths conceal both fear and grace,
An endless void, a secret place.

Beneath the waves, time drifts away,
A dance of light, the dreams at play.
With every tide, the echoes bloom,
In darkened depths, we face our doom.

In the Depths of Whispered Dreams

In quiet corners of the night,
Secrets slumber, out of sight.
A gentle breeze, a fleeting thought,
In whispered dreams, our solace sought.

Softly now, the shadows creep,
Enticing visions, lure us deep.
In tranquil realms, our spirits soar,
Embracing what lies at the core.

The Serpent's Lullaby

With scales that shimmer, voices low,
The serpent sings, a trance-like flow.
Embraced by night, as stars ignite,
Its lullaby enchants the light.

In depths unseen, where fears reside,
It beckons close, a tempting guide.
To dance with dreams, with fate entwined,
A song of shadows, intertwined.

Faint Light Beneath the Surface

A flicker glows in darkened seas,
A hint of hope that stirs the breeze.
Drawing near, the light will guide,
To shores unknown, where dreams abide.

Beneath the waves, the heart will yearn,
For mysteries that softly burn.
With every step, the shadows wane,
As faint light breaks the cold domain.

Silhouettes of Possibility

In dawn's soft glow we stand,
Chasing dreams we can't yet see,
Whispers of the future call,
Hope entwined with mystery.

Footsteps echo on the road,
Paths of light and shadows play,
Each choice a shimmering thread,
Weaving fate in bright array.

With every turn, a chance awaits,
New horizons stretch their wings,
In the silence, visions bloom,
Life's song softly rises, sings.

Together we embrace the day,
With hearts unbound, we soar and glide,
Silhouettes of possibility,
In endless skies, our dreams reside.

Shimmers in the Void

In the depth of night we gaze,
Stars like diamonds pierce the dark,
Whispers of the cosmos flow,
Each shimmer holds a tiny spark.

Lost in cosmos, hearts embrace,
Galaxies dance in silent song,
Time transcends in gentle waves,
Infinity, where we belong.

In the void, we find our truth,
Every moment, a fleeting breath,
Connection threads, unseen but strong,
In shimmers, we defy the death.

Hold my hand as we explore,
The mysteries of endless night,
For in darkness, we find light,
Shimmers guide our hearts in flight.

Intrigue in the Darkness

In shadows deep, we weave our tales,
Secrets hidden, voices low,
Each glance exchanged speaks volumes loud,
In darkness, sparks of interest grow.

Intrigue dances on the edge,
Where curiosity ignites,
Layers unfold, a puzzle grand,
Keepers of elusive sights.

With whispered truths and silent vows,
We navigate this cryptic space,
Every heartbeat feels like fate,
A thrilling chase, a timeless race.

In the dark, connections bloom,
Mysteries bind as shadows twine,
Each step lends a new resolve,
Intrigue pulls, and souls align.

The Veil of Mystery

A curtain drawn, the night descends,
Veils of shadow cloak the light,
Questions linger in the air,
Wrapped in whispers, out of sight.

What tales lie beneath the silk?
What dreams rest in the quiet hush?
Every secret cloaked in time,
Yearning hearts, the silent crush.

In the distance, echoes call,
Each sound a clue to what may be,
The veil lifts, for just a breath,
Uncovering paths that set us free.

Through the mist of the unknown,
We dance with hope, and fears, and joy,
The veil of mystery entwined,
Life's enchantments to enjoy.

Lightyearing into the Unfathomable

Stars beckon from endless night,
Galaxies swirl in cosmic flight.
Time stretches, bends, and sways,
Lightyearing through the vast arrays.

Dreams collide in the ether's glow,
Whispers of worlds we yearn to know.
In silence, we traverse the void,
Infinity—both feared and enjoyed.

The pulse of the universe sings,
A melody of celestial things.
With every leap through starry bed,
We chase what the cosmos has said.

Resonance of Untold Stories

In shadows where secrets sleep,
Echoes of hearts begin to weep.
Voices linger in the air,
Tales of love, loss, and despair.

Each watchful silence holds a dream,
Rippling soft like a gentle stream.
Yearning whispers fill the night,
Resonance of time lost from sight.

Weaving threads of joy and pain,
Binding us in an unseen chain.
Every narrative finds a way,
To dance in the light of day.

Hues of the Unspeakable

Colors bleed through whispered sighs,
A spectrum that never dies.
Shadows waltz in twilight's embrace,
Hues of the unspeakable trace.

In every brush, a story spun,
Underneath the fading sun.
Imagined realms take on a form,
Beauty and chaos forever warm.

Crimson dreams with azure skies,
Violet truths beneath the lies.
Artistry born from silent screams,
Reflects the essence of our dreams.

Reflections from the Abyss

In depths where sunlight cannot breach,
Secrets lie just out of reach.
Mirrors crack and shadows crawl,
Reflections from the abyss call.

Each gaze deeper than the last,
Wisdom forms from the silent past.
An echo from the darkened sea,
Inviting us to simply be.

With every ripple in the dark,
Sparks of truth ignite a spark.
What we fear may lead us home,
In the depths, we are never alone.

Beneath the Mask of Night

Stars whisper secrets, bright and bold,
The moon cradles dreams, quiet yet told.
Shadows dance softly on the ground,
In the stillness, lost thoughts abound.

Night unveils beauty, so calm and deep,
While the world outside prepares for sleep.
Cloaked in silence, hearts take flight,
Finding solace beneath the mask of night.

A breeze carries tales of ancient lore,
Echoes of laughter from times before.
Hope glimmers faintly with each breath,
Beneath night's veil, life conquers death.

In the loom of darkness, we make our vows,
Under the watchful gaze of the owls.
Love's promise entwines with the stars,
Beneath the night, we venture far.

Breaths of Untold Stories

In every heartbeat lies a quest,
A saga waiting to be expressed.
Voices murmur softly in the air,
Tales of sorrow, joy, and despair.

Years invade the quiet of the mind,
Leaving whispers of the lives we find.
Each breath a chapter, each sigh a theme,
Untold stories woven in a dream.

Underneath the surface, currents flow,
Revelations waiting, yet to show.
Listen closely, let the silence talk,
In breaths of time, the past will walk.

Every gaze exchanged holds a fate,
Unraveled threads tied by chance and fate.
In the tapestry of souls, we learn,
Breaths of stories ignite and burn.

A Light Within the Mist

Fog gently blankets the sleeping earth,
Hiding the treasures that hold their worth.
A flicker appears, piercing the gray,
A beacon of hope on a clouded day.

Winds of change dance through the air,
Carrying whispers, fragile and rare.
Within the mist, a glow begins,
Promising warmth as the journey spins.

Steps take form through the veils of time,
Guided by dreams through shadows that climb.
With every heartbeat, courage unfolds,
A light within the mist, brave and bold.

Together we wander through uncharted space,
Tracing the light as it leads the chase.
In the murkiness, we've come to exist,
Finding our path, wrapped in the mist.

The Enigma of Silence

In stillness, mystery finds its grace,
Words unspoken, weaves a lace.
The heart beats loudly in the void,
Echoing dreams once destroyed.

Silence, an ocean, vast and deep,
In its depths, lost secrets keep.
It whispers truths that words may hide,
In the quiet, shadows abide.

Between the breaths, tension resides,
Holding timelines where fate decides.
Moments linger, precious and rare,
In the enigma, we find our share.

Listen closely to the silence hum,
In its rhythm, we all become.
With every pause, revelation sparks,
In the silence, we ignite our arcs.

Secrets in the Starlit Veil

Whispers low in the night,
Stars writing tales of old.
Each twinkling spark, a light,
Unfolding mysteries untold.

In shadows cast by the moon,
Dreams linger like fragrant blooms.
They dance to a silent tune,
Filling the air with their plumes.

Guardians of the midnight glow,
Timeless secrets they conceal.
In their depths, the stories flow,
A tapestry they reveal.

Embrace the wonders of night,
Let the starlight guide your way.
Within the dark, there's pure light,
Eternal is their ballet.

The Dance of Forgotten Dreams

In corners where shadows meet,
Old echoes start to sing.
Forgotten dreams on silent feet,
Awaken to the night's soft spring.

They twirl beneath the silver skies,
Lost wishes weave through the trees.
Soft laughter and distant sighs,
Flow gently with the evening breeze.

A waltz of hopes, long unclaimed,
Entwines with the heartbeat of night.
Each step, a vision, unnamed,
Filling the dark with delight.

They beckon, these dreams of yore,
With whispers both sweet and rare.
In twilight's embrace, they soar,
Spreading their wings in the air.

Flickers in the Darkened Sky

Glimmers dance like fireflies,
In the vast expanse of night.
Hope ignites as darkness sighs,
Stars awaken, shining bright.

A canvas deep, a void of peace,
Where silence holds its breath so tight.
Each flicker grants the soul release,
An echo of forgotten light.

Moments lost in time's embrace,
Fleeting as the passing wind.
They paint the sky with silent grace,
Stories that the night rescind.

In each blink, a world anew,
Reflecting dreams that we once sought.
These flickers guide me back to you,
Through the shadows, hope is caught.

Revelations of the Unseen

In shadows, truths softly weave,
Secrets linger, pure and wise.
With every heart that dares believe,
Unspoken tales begin to rise.

In stillness, the dawn reveals,
The whispered words of ancient lore.
Each lesson that the silence seals,
Awakens what we must explore.

The unseen threads of fate entwine,
Connecting paths that we have lost.
Every heartbeat, a sacred sign,
Guides us gently, no matter the cost.

Embrace the quiet, the profound,
For within lies a world divine.
In silence, let your soul be found,
In revelations that brightly shine.

Dance of Shadows

In the twilight's gentle sigh,
Figures sway, they spin and fly,
Whispers woven into night,
Shadows dance in silver light.

Fingers trace the edges deep,
Where the secrets safely keep,
In the hush, they breathe, they play,
In the dark, they steal away.

Silent echoes call and gleam,
Lost within a waking dream,
They tilt, they turn without a sound,
In their grace, the night is found.

With each step, the night holds tight,
Veil of stars, a jeweled sight,
Shadows blend, then slip and part,
In the dance, we find the heart.

Glowing Fragments of Time

Moments flicker like bright sparks,
In the dark, they leave their marks,
Whispers of what once has been,
Glowing softly, pure and keen.

Each tick carries a star's breath,
Painting tales of life and death,
In the stillness, stories grow,
Fragments of the world's soft glow.

Shadows stretch, then fade away,
As dawn brings the light of day,
Yet their warmth, though far and near,
Holds a truth we long to hear.

Memories dance in twilight's embrace,
Carried forth at a gentle pace,
In each heartbeat, time's design,
Patterns weave, and stars align.

The Other Side of Twilight

Where dusk meets the waiting stars,
Lies a place beyond our scars,
Veils of night whisper and sway,
Guiding souls who've lost their way.

In shadows soft, a truth unwinds,
The echoes of our searching minds,
Across the edge, they beckon clear,
To the heart, where dreams reappear.

Past the horizon, colors blend,
In silence, we begin to mend,
Holding close the light that fades,
Bridges built from love's charades.

On the other side, stars still gleam,
Sparks of hope in every dream,
Where the night and day collide,
In this space, our souls abide.

Secrets in the Moonlight

Beneath the silver's tender glow,
Ancient tales begin to flow,
In the night, soft whispers rise,
Secrets known to midnight skies.

Each shimmering beam holds a sigh,
Of wishes cast, and dreams that fly,
In the quiet, hearts unfold,
Revealing stories long untold.

The moon's embrace, a silent guide,
With every pulse, we bide our time,
Hiding truths in shadows' care,
Yearning souls find solace there.

In the depths of night's embrace,
Finding warmth in empty space,
With each glance, we softly see,
Secrets shared, for you and me.

Radiance of the Unexplored

In shadows deep, a beacon glows,
A whisper calls where no one goes.
With every step, the darkness fades,
In newfound light, the heart invades.

The air is thick with dreams untold,
Adventure waits for the brave and bold.
Each hidden path, a story unfolds,
In the quiet night, a world beholds.

Mysteries dance in moonlit grace,
With every heartbeat, time takes place.
The soul ignites in vivid hues,
Embracing all, with nothing to lose.

Through valleys vast and peaks so high,
The spirit soars, as if to fly.
In every glance, the wonders gleam,
In radiance bright, we chase the dream.

Translucent Echoes

Beneath the waves, a whisper sings,
The heart of ocean, a world of things.
In fragile shades of blue and green,
Translucent echoes softly glean.

The light cascades through watery veils,
With gentle strokes, each ripple trails.
Secrets murmur in the tide,
In silken swells, the dreams abide.

Every note a story we weave,
In currents deep, we dare believe.
With every glance, the visions spark,
In twilight's glow, we leave our mark.

Through time we flow, a ceaseless stream,
In twilight's touch, the shadows beam.
Translucent echoes, a timeless grace,
In heartbeats shared, we find our place.

Threads of the Uncharted

A tapestry of paths unknown,
In woven whispers, dreams are sown.
Each thread a journey, rich and bold,
In uncharted lands, stories unfold.

With nimble hands, we stitch the seams,
In every color, we chase our dreams.
The fabric shifts, the patterns change,
Through tangled trails, we rearrange.

In laughter bright and silent tears,
We gather strength, confront our fears.
Each intersection, a spark ignites,
In woven hearts, our hope ignites.

The unseen map, our guiding light,
In storms we sail, through darkest night.
Threads of the uncharted, our embrace,
In every journey, we find our place.

Beyond the Known Depths

In silent depths, the echoes call,
To venture forth, to risk our all.
The ocean's heart, a siren's song,
In unknown waters, we belong.

With courage steeled, we dive anew,
To chase the dreams we thought we knew.
In swirling currents, fear takes flight,
Beyond the known, we find our light.

In shadows deep, we chase the dawn,
With every pulse, a spirit drawn.
The depths reveal what's yet to see,
In boundless waves, we learn to be.

In uncharted skies, our vessels soar,
The heart's adventure forevermore.
Beyond the known depths, the treasures gleam,
In every whisper, we find our dream.

Intangible Presences at Dusk

Whispers linger on the breeze,
Shadows dance beneath the trees.
Colors fade, the day withdraws,
Night unveils her hidden flaws.

Footsteps echo, soft and light,
Glimmers spark in fading light.
Nature breathes a gentle sigh,
As the stars begin to pry.

Murmurs weave through thickening air,
Mysteries linger everywhere.
In the twilight's soft embrace,
We find solace, a quiet place.

Voices of the past resound,
In the twilight, silence found.
Every moment stretches thin,
In the dusk, our dreams begin.

Riddles in the Midnight Air

Shivering winds carry tales of old,
Secrets whispered in the cold.
Moonlight casts its silver sheen,
On the mysteries yet unseen.

Stars conspire, their patterns tease,
Drawing maps that hint with ease.
In the stillness, questions rise,
Riddles held in shadowed skies.

Silent echoes beckon near,
Voices faint, yet crystal clear.
What was lost, and what remains,
In the midnight's open veins?

Thoughts entwined like twinkling lights,
Illuminating inner flights.
Within these hours, truth may glean,
Whatever lies beneath the sheen.

The Beauty of the Unexplored

Beyond the trails of well-trod feet,
Lies a world both wild and sweet.
Mountains loom, untamed, vast,
Hiding wonders unsurpassed.

Rivers carve their ancient paths,
In silent lull, the forest brats.
Every corner blooms with chance,
Inviting all to seek, to dance.

Decay composes nature's song,
Where even broken things belong.
Birds take flight in crisp, clear air,
To distant lands from here to there.

In the whispers of the trees,
Life unfolds with perfect ease.
The unexplored, a siren's call,
Inviting every heart to enthrall.

Unwritten Pages in the Dark

Empty sheets await the ink,
In the silence, thoughts will sink.
Quiet moments, ripe and bare,
Whispers of a story rare.

Night enfolds the world in black,
Dreams take form, leave no track.
Only echoes, soft and deep,
In shadows where our secrets keep.

Pages turn with breathless grace,
Each new line carves out a space.
What the dawn will bring within,
Lies hidden where the night has been.

Each blank slate a chance to start,
With every word, we bare our heart.
In the dark, potential shines,
Unwritten tales, our fate aligns.

The Unseen Horizon

Beyond the edge of sight, we yearn,
Where time and dreams entwine, we learn.
A whisper calls from distant shore,
Awakening hearts to seek for more.

In twilight's glow, the shadows play,
Unfolding secrets of the day.
With every step, the path unfolds,
A tapestry of stories told.

The stars align, a guiding light,
Through tangled woods and endless night.
With faith as sails, we brave the sea,
To chase horizons, wild and free.

So let us wander, hand in hand,
Across the realms of time's vast land.
For in the journey, truth resides,
The unseen horizon ever hides.

Flickers of Forgotten Paths

In the quiet dusk, memories gleam,
Flickers of dreams that once were deemed.
Footsteps echo in the fading light,
Whispers of hopes lost to the night.

Through tangled woods, we search in vain,
For traces of laughter, love, and pain.
Each leaf that falls bears tales untold,
Of journeys taken, brave and bold.

Stars above, they watch and sigh,
For every path we let slip by.
Yet in the heart, they softly glow,
Flickers of paths we used to know.

So take a breath, let go of fears,
Embrace the past, the joy, the tears.
For though the roads may twist and part,
The flickers linger in the heart.

Illumination in the Abyss

In the depth of night, shadows creep,
Awakening secrets that darkness keeps.
Yet through the void, a spark ignites,
Bringing forth hope in the coldest nights.

A candle's flame against the chill,
Illumination strong, a quiet thrill.
For even in depths, where silence reigns,
Resilience blooms, despite the pains.

With every breath, the darkness wanes,
Guiding us through our deepest chains.
For as we sink, we learn to rise,
Finding strength beneath the skies.

So let the light within you swell,
For even in depths, we craft our spell.
Through the abyss, we will ascend,
Illumination, our truest friend.

Veiled Journeys

Beneath a shroud of mist and dreams,
Veiled journeys dwell in silent streams.
With every step, the unknown calls,
Whispers of fate as twilight falls.

In shadows cast by candle's glow,
Paths unseen, yet ours to know.
Each twist and turn, a tale anew,
In hidden realms, our spirits flew.

Through forests deep, and mountains high,
We traverse time, the earth, the sky.
With hearts wide open, we take the leap,
Into the veils, where secrets sleep.

So hold my hand, and let's explore,
The journeys veiled, forevermore.
For in the silence, truth shall bloom,
In veiled journeys, find our room.

The Charm of Uncharted Waters

In whispers soft, the waters call,
Their secrets dance, both grand and small.
Beneath the waves, a world unseen,
Awaits the brave, the hearts serene.

With every tide, a story flows,
Of sunlit dreams and starry woes.
The charm of depths, both wild and free,
Invites the soul to wander, see.

Oh, navigate with gentle grace,
As currents lead to hidden space.
In uncharted realms, we find our truth,
A vibrant spark of timeless youth.

So sail we on, through night and day,
To realms where hope will always stay.
Embrace the thrill of the unknown,
In water's heart, we find our home.

Echoes of the Unheld

In shadows deep, the whispers dwell,
The stories sung, yet none can tell.
Yearnings filled with a silent grace,
Echoes linger in empty space.

For every touch that slipped away,
A memory lingers, soft as clay.
The unheld dreams we dared to weave,
In quiet moments, we still believe.

Like autumn leaves that drift and sway,
Our hearts recall what time won't fray.
In fragments lost, yet still intact,
Resounding notes that we attract.

In midnight hours, when thoughts collide,
We seek the warmth where love might bide.
For echoes buzz, a tender thread,
Binding the things we left unsaid.

Inkblots of What Lies Beneath

On paper white, in ink we play,
Doodles dance in a vibrant array.
With splashes bold and lines that bend,
Unlocking dreams we cannot end.

Each blot reveals a hidden tale,
Of whispered thoughts that oft set sail.
What lies beneath, we strive to know,
In every stroke, our feelings flow.

Emotions bleed on pages worn,
In hues of dusk, where hopes are born.
We sketch our fears in graphite shade,
In inkblots bright, our truths cascaded.

Let chaos bloom on every sheet,
As heartbeats blend with lines discreet.
In every mess, a work of art,
Inkblots tell the stories of the heart.

The Glow of an Invisible Cosmos

In silent night, the stars ignite,
A vast expanse of pure delight.
The glow unseen, yet felt so clear,
An infinite dance we long to hear.

Celestial dreams, beyond our sight,
Whisk us away through endless night.
In every glimmer, a spark of grace,
An invisible cosmos, an endless space.

With whispered winds, the heavens sigh,
Inviting souls to touch the sky.
In cosmic tides, our fates entwined,
Through eons past, and love defined.

So let us gaze with open hearts,
To where the universe imparts.
In stardust trails, we find our way,
The glow of hope, forever stay.

The Language of Vague Echoes

In whispers of the night, they call,
Shadows dance, they rise and fall.
Words unspoken linger near,
Fragments of thoughts that disappear.

Upon the breeze, they softly sigh,
Mysteries hidden beneath the sky.
Each echo weaves a tale unknown,
In silence, truth finds its own tone.

Through twilight's veil, they intertwine,
A tapestry of fate divine.
Listen close to what they say,
In the language of night, they play.

With every sound, a secret shared,
In fleeting moments, hearts laid bare.
So linger here, let dreams unfold,
In vague echoes, stories told.

Mirage of the Enchanted Woods

In the heart of the woods where shadows lie,
A shimmering veil catches the eye.
Whispers of magic dance on the breeze,
Yet step with caution beneath the trees.

Light filters through the ancient boughs,
Creating visions that time allows.
A river of dreams, an echoing sound,
In this realm of wonder, lost can be found.

Colors that shift in the fading light,
Flickers of beauty in the depths of night.
Mirrors of water that reflect the sky,
In this enchanted world, let spirits fly.

But beware the path that seems too clear,
For mirages mislead, instilling fear.
Yet brave the heart that seeks the good,
For treasure lies deep in the enchanted wood.

Velvet Paths of Possibility

Soft as the night, these paths unfold,
A journey of dreams, in whispers told.
Each step we take, a choice anew,
On velvet trails, where hopes break through.

Midst twilight hues, they gently glow,
A tapestry of futures, ebb and flow.
Invite the stars to guide our way,
As shadows lift, and dusk turns to day.

Echoes of laughter, hearts intertwine,
Lost in the beauty of the divine.
Within each moment, the world expands,
Through velvet paths, we take our stands.

Embrace the chance, these roads bestow,
For hidden treasures lie in the flow.
Where dreams unite, possibilities gleam,
On velvet paths, we weave our dream.

Flickering Hope in Dusk

As daylight wanes, the shadows creep,
In whispers soft, our secrets keep.
Yet in the dark, a light will glow,
Flickering hope through the dusk will show.

Stars appear, like distant friends,
Reminders that every story blends.
Though night may fall and fears arise,
Hope's gentle flicker lights the skies.

In the soft embrace of twilight's hue,
Dreams and wishes can still come true.
For every end holds a hidden start,
In flickering hope, we find our heart.

So hold on tight as darkness falls,
For in that space, a new voice calls.
With every flicker, the dawn will break,
Hope is the path that we shall take.

Hints of Magic in the Mundane

In the quiet hum of dawn,
Birds whisper tunes to the trees.
A flicker of light, a fleeting smile,
Life dances softly in the breeze.

Coffee steam swirls like spells,
Each drop a tale left undone.
Weaving dreams in the simplest things,
The extraordinary in everyone.

Cracks in the pavement shimmer bright,
As if holding secrets so dear.
Amid dust and noise, magic thrives,
Waiting for hearts to draw near.

Lost in routine's gentle embrace,
The world reveals its quiet grace.
Hints of magic come out to play,
Transforming night into day.

The Pulse of the Unimagined

Beneath the surface, rhythms beat,
Echoes of dreams yet found.
The stars above weave stories deep,
In silence, possibilities abound.

Moments collide in rich embrace,
Where visions twist and entwine.
Every heartbeat writes the script,
Of tales waiting to shine.

Fingers trace the edge of fate,
In shadows, the future sings.
An unseen world begs to be known,
Amongst the everyday things.

Dive into the depths of thought,
Each pulse a journey, uncharted.
In the unimagined lies the spark,
That ignites the dreams we started.

Secrets Cradled by Shadows

In twilight's hold, whispers grow,
Secrets wrapped in ancient lore.
The moonlight weaves a silken path,
Leading to what was before.

Figures dance in soft delight,
Crafted from nothing but haze.
Each corner breathes a mystery,
Captured in the night's embrace.

Echoes linger, soft and low,
Tales of love and fears once shared.
In the silence, shadows speak,
Unraveling what's long been bared.

Find the truths in dusk's caress,
Where memories and dreams reside.
In shadows' arms, secrets rest,
A world where wonders abide.

Breaths of the Untold

In every sigh, a story sleeps,
Waiting for moments to unfold.
Each breath a journey, soft yet bold,
Carrying whispers of the old.

The cracks in the earth hold hints of time,
Heartbeats lost in the wild.
Every wind's gust has a tale to share,
In nature's arms, we're all a child.

With every step, horizons shift,
Paths converge and collide.
In the tapestry of life, we find,
Breaths of the untold are our guide.

Echoed in laughter, pain, and peace,
Stories linger, yearning to be.
In the quiet moments, they take flight,
Awakening what's yet to be.

Hidden Lanterns

In the dark of night, they shine,
Flickering softly, a gentle sign.
Guiding souls through the unknown,
Whispers of light, they have grown.

Among the shadows, they dance and sway,
Unseen by many, yet never stray.
Each glow a story, a tale untold,
In hidden corners, they break the mold.

They flicker hopes, they spark delight,
Encouraging dreams to take flight.
Invisible hands, they beckon near,
These hidden lanterns, they hold us dear.

When the world seems lost in despair,
Their warm embrace, a breath of air.
A constellation of faith and grace,
In every heart, they find a place.

A Spectrum of Secrets

In colors bright, they softly gleam,
Each hue a truth, a silent dream.
Hidden whispers in every shade,
A spectrum of secrets, never delayed.

Reds of passion, deep and bold,
Greens of envy, stories told.
Blues of sorrow, calm and deep,
In every color, a secret to keep.

The canvas of life, richly drawn,
With strokes of mystery at the dawn.
Every shade a life embraced,
In the heart's spectrum, secrets traced.

Unraveled threads of tales so bold,
In hidden hues, their stories unfold.
A dance of colors in the light,
A spectrum of secrets, burning bright.

In the Wake of Uncertainty

Waves crash hard upon the shore,
Echoes of doubt, we can't ignore.
Tides of change pull us away,
In the wake of uncertainty, we sway.

Footsteps falter on shifting sand,
As we reach out for a guiding hand.
Foggy visions cloud our mind,
In the wake of uncertainty, we're blind.

Yet in the chaos, there's a spark,
A glimmer of light in the dark.
Navigating paths unknown, we find,
In the wake of uncertainty, we're kind.

Resilience grows in every heart,
From scattered pieces, we make art.
Though storms may rage and fears ignite,
In the wake of uncertainty, we find light.

The Hidden Luminary

Hidden away in shadows cast,
A luminary shines steadfast.
Though unseen by most who roam,
In quiet corners, they find home.

Guiding whispers through the night,
Changing paths with subtle light.
A silent guardian, ever near,
The hidden luminary, holding dear.

In moments of doubt, they arise,
A beacon bright in twilight skies.
Their glow reminds us not to fear,
The hidden luminary is always here.

In the stillness, they softly call,
Echoing truths that encompass all.
From depths unseen, they help us see,
The hidden luminary, setting us free.

Encounters with the Phantom Light

In the hush of night, whispers call,
Ghostly beams in twilight fall.
Shapes that shimmer, dance with grace,
Fleeting shadows, I embrace.

They beckon softly, secrets share,
A flicker here, a phantom's flare.
Mysterious paths in silence glide,
Illuminated by the tide.

Yet as I reach, they slip away,
Illusive dreams that softly sway.
In stillness caught, the world feels light,
A fleeting waltz with phantom light.

Each encounter leaves a trace,
A lasting kiss, a hidden space.
In memory's glow, they take flight,
These ethereal whispers of the night.

Shades of Curiosity and Wonder

Beneath the surface, questions brew,
A palette rich, in shades anew.
Colors blend, horizon's kiss,
Crafting dreams within the mist.

A child's gaze, so wide, so bright,
Sees the world in pure delight.
Each step a marvel, every sound,
In each moment, magic found.

Through the woods, where stories play,
Curious hearts chase night and day.
Each leaf a secret, each stone a song,
A journey where we all belong.

In twilight's embrace, we ponder still,
Wonders vast on the emerald hill.
Curiosity, a guiding star,
In every shadow, treasures are.

A Serenade of the Unseen

In whispers soft, beyond the veil,
Lies a tune, a haunting trail.
Echoes linger, unseen charm,
A melody, wrapped in calm.

Notes that flutter in the air,
Bring to life the things we share.
Fleeting glimpses, a knowing glance,
Unseen threads of fate's own dance.

As dusk descends, shadows entwine,
In concert with the stars that shine.
Brushing against the edge of dreams,
Life's serenade softly beams.

To listen closely, heartbeats play,
In the silence, love finds its way.
An unseen force, a gentle guide,
In every heart, forever resides.

Chronicles of Fading Moments

Time etches tales on weary hands,
Moments slip like fleeting sands.
Each sigh a story, every glance,
Chronicles of a lost romance.

Pages turn, and shadows wane,
In laughter's echo, joys remain.
Yet as each chapter fades from sight,
Memories linger, soft and bright.

In twilight's glow, we pause and reflect,
Cherished times we won't neglect.
A dance of seconds, heartbeats fleet,
In every heartbeat, life's heartbeat.

The past a tapestry we weave,
In fading moments, we believe.
A journey held in tender light,
Chronicles of love taking flight.

The Unraveled Thread

In time's embrace, the colors fade,
A tapestry of choices made.
Threads of joy, and strands of woe,
Woven tight, then pulled to show.

Each knot a story, softly told,
Of dreams and fears, both brave and bold.
Yet with a tug, they come undone,
A journey's end, a race not run.

Frayed edges whisper secrets near,
Of laughter lost, and hidden fear.
The fabric worn, yet still it gleams,
In all that's lost, are half-formed dreams.

Rewoven hopes in shadows cast,
Threads of the future, tied to the past.
An intricate dance, a fragile thread,
In every end, a new road bred.

Fragments of What Was Never Seen

In quiet corners where shadows creep,
Whispers linger, memories steep.
Fragments dance in the dimming light,
Unraveled tales of lost delight.

The unseen truths, like ghosts they roam,
In every heart, a silent home.
Faded echoes of dreams once bold,
Stories untold, forever hold.

Through veils of time, they seek to speak,
Beneath the surface, soft and weak.
The pieces scattered, far and wide,
A puzzle made of worlds inside.

In every glance, a spark remains,
In each lost moment, lingering pains.
What never was, still feels so clear,
In the silence, all we hold dear.

Sirens in the Mist

Through swirling fog, their voices call,
Melodies beguile, a siren's thrall.
With haunting tones that pierce the night,
They beckon souls to take their flight.

In shadows deep, the echoes soar,
A dance of fate along the shore.
The mist conceals their fleeting grace,
Each note a touch, a soft embrace.

Yet caution lies within their song,
For not all trails lead where they belong.
With hearts entangled, lost in dreams,
They weave a web from silvered seams.

When dawn breaks through, the sirens fade,
But in our hearts, their dreams invade.
A haunting chord, forever stays,
In whispered winds, their magic plays.

Echoes of Forgotten Memories

In twilight's grasp, the echoes fade,
Of laughter shared, and promises made.
Each moment lost, a fleeting sigh,
In dusty corners where shadows lie.

Unearthed again, like old love letters,
In fragile folds, the heart confers.
Whispers linger on the breeze,
Soft reminders that tease and please.

Reflections dance in the moonlit stream,
Fleeting flashes of a dream.
Yet in the depths of fading light,
We find the strength to hold them tight.

Through hazy nights, their warmth remains,
In every heart, a touch of pain.
Yet still, we cherish what we've lost,
For echoes persist, whatever the cost.

Shimmering in the Peripheral

In twilight's grace, shadows play,
A whisper of light fades away,
Dreams dance in the edge of sight,
Glimmers of hope in the falling night.

Stars weave tales in cosmic streams,
Awakening thoughts, hidden dreams,
In the quiet, magic swirls,
Unveiling secrets of hidden worlds.

The journey's call lies on the breeze,
Softly stirring ancient trees,
Where the unseen beckons near,
Inviting hearts to draw it clear.

In the periphery, we find our spark,
Casting shadows in the dark,
With every sigh, we dive anew,
Into the shimmering, out of view.

The Enigma of Lost Horizons

Beyond the realm of what we know,
Lies a mystery that ebbs and flows,
In the echoes of forgotten calls,
Where ancient wisdom gently falls.

The sun dips low, painting the skies,
A canvas filled with whispered sighs,
Horizons shift, a dance untold,
Secrets wrapped in threads of gold.

We chase the light, yet find the shade,
In the labyrinth of dreams we wade,
Each step forward, a leap of faith,
In the enigma, we find our wraith.

Lost horizons guide the way,
With each dusk, we're led astray,
Yet in the weaving of time's embrace,
There's beauty hidden in every trace.

Veils of Time and Silence

In the hush of nightfall's glow,
Time wraps us in its gentle flow,
Veils of silence drape the land,
A soothing touch from nature's hand.

Memories linger in the mist,
Each moment shared, too sweet to resist,
The heartbeat echoes through the years,
A tapestry spun from laughter and tears.

Cloaked in shadows, the past resides,
Guarding secrets where wisdom hides,
In stillness, voices softly blend,
A chorus of whispers that never end.

Through veils of time, we journey wide,
In the arms of silence, we confide,
For in each breath, a story lives,
And in each heart, a promise gives.

Echoing in the Labyrinth

Winding paths through twisted halls,
Where shadows flicker and mystery calls,
Each step we take leads us astray,
In the labyrinth where echoes sway.

Voices murmur through ancient stone,
In the maze, we wander alone,
Seeking meaning in fragmented light,
Hoping to find a way to ignite.

The walls remember what time forgot,
Each corner turned, a lesson taught,
With every turn, a heartbeat draws,
A compass forged in hidden laws.

In echoes sharp, we find our way,
Through the dark, into the gray,
For the labyrinth holds a truth profound,
In its riddle, life's essence is found.

Whispers in the Shadows

In the night, the whispers creep,
Secrets hidden, dreams to keep.
Voices soft, like distant chimes,
Calling forth forgotten times.

Beneath the moon's pale, silver light,
Shadows dance in silent flight.
Echoes of what used to be,
A faint trace of memory.

Within the stillness, hearts unfold,
Tales of warmth and stories told.
In the dark, a spark ignites,
Whispers weaving through the nights.

Listen close, the night confides,
In the shadows, truth abides.
Every sigh and fleeting glance,
Fuels the night's enchanting dance.

Secrets Beneath the Surface

Beneath the waves, the secrets lie,
In the depths, where whispers sigh.
Hidden tales of time and tide,
In this world, wonders abide.

Ripples carry dreams untold,
In the depths, the brave and bold.
Mystical realms, where shadows play,
Guarded truths, kept far away.

In the silence, treasures gleam,
Secrets waiting for a dream.
Secrets waiting, patient, still,
Yearning hearts, with hope to fill.

Dive with courage, take the plunge,
In the depths, passions lunge.
Find the whispers, soft and sweet,
Secrets waiting to be complete.

Echoes of Hidden Dreams

In the silence, echoes rise,
Hidden dreams in shadowed skies.
A distant call, a fleeting thought,
Memories of the battles fought.

In twilight's glow, the dreams unfold,
Secrets woven, brave and bold.
Each whisper, like a gentle breeze,
Carries hopes through timeless seas.

Listen close, let the echoes sway,
Guide your heart, come what may.
In the stillness, find the light,
Illuminating darkest night.

With every heartbeat, dreams revive,
In echoes, we learn to thrive.
Together, we chase the gleam,
Forever caught in hidden dreams.

Luminous Veils

In the dawn, the veils ignite,
Colors bloom in morning light.
Softly drawn, the curtains fade,
Unveiling beauty, dreams portrayed.

Through the mist, a silhouette,
Luminous, we can't forget.
Every hue a story spun,
Ripples dance as day's begun.

In fragile light, the veils entwine,
Secrets wrapped, so divine.
With every shimmer, hearts align,
In the glow, our souls combine.

Lift the veil, let visions sing,
In the light, all hope takes wing.
Luminous paths for us to roam,
In the veils, we find our home.

The Hidden Sanctuary

In the heart of the wood, silence sings,
Where ancient trees spread their wings.
Shadows dance on the forest floor,
A secret place to explore.

Moss carpets the ground, soft and green,
A sanctuary where dreams convene.
Whispers of wind tell stories untold,
In this refuge, mysteries unfold.

Rays of sunlight weave through the leaves,
Painting patterns, where the heart believes.
In the embrace of nature's hold,
The hidden sanctuary, a treasure of gold.

Beneath the stars, the night descends,
Here in solitude, the spirit mends.
With every breath, peace draws near,
In the hidden sanctuary,, love is clear.

Mysteries of the Star-Studded Sky

Beneath the cloak of the velvet night,
Stars shimmer softly, a wondrous sight.
Each one a tale, a distant dream,
Whispers of cosmos, a celestial theme.

The moon stands guard, a glowing guide,
Unveiling secrets that long abide.
Constellations weave a timeless song,
In the vastness, where we belong.

Twinkles of light in endless black,
Echoes of ages that never lack.
In this realm of ancient lore,
We ponder the mysteries evermore.

Caught in a trance, we gaze up high,
Lost in the depth of the star-studded sky.
Each shining beacon a wish in flight,
Leading our hearts through the silent night.

The Call of the Unfamiliar

In the distance, a whisper calls,
A siren song as twilight falls.
Paths untaken, a beckoning light,
Drawing the eager into the night.

Waves of change crash on the shore,
A taste of adventure, we long for more.
Fear and thrill dance hand in hand,
Together we step, on uncharted land.

Each shadow holds a mystery dear,
In every corner, the unknown near.
With open hearts, we embrace the strange,
For in the unfamiliar, life can change.

The road may twist, the journey long,
But the call of the unfamiliar is strong.
In the unknown, we find our way,
With courage to dream, we seize the day.

Neither Here Nor There

Between the worlds, a thin line stands,
A place where time slips through our hands.
Neither here nor there, we drift in dreams,
A tapestry woven with silent seams.

Echoes of laughter, shadows of past,
Moments we treasure, never meant to last.
In the liminal space, we find our rest,
A gentle pause, in life's great quest.

Footsteps lingering on the edge of time,
Caught in the rhythm, a haunting rhyme.
In this twilight, we pause and stare,
Finding our balance, neither here nor there.

Memories swirl like leaves in the air,
In this in-between, we shed our care.
Through the veil, we embrace the night,
In the realm of shadows, we find our light.

Signs from the Unfathomable

Beneath the stars, whispers swirl,
Ancient tales in shadows unfurl.
Eclipsed by the night, they call,
Fragments of time, in silence, fall.

Hidden truths, in dark they weave,
Echoes of dreams that we believe.
A constellation's soft embrace,
Guides the seeker to a place.

Veiled in mist, the paths unfold,
Every heartbeat, a story told.
In the void, where lost things dwell,
Signs emerge, a secret spell.

With every breath, the mystery grows,
A symphony of life that flows.
In the unfathomable deep,
Awakened souls begin to leap.

The Allure of Silent Nightscapes

In twilight's hush, the world slows down,
Stars awaken, wear their crown.
Moonlit paths, they softly glow,
Guiding dreams where shadows flow.

The night whispers to the trees,
Carried gently by the breeze.
Echoes dance in stillness' grace,
Every breath, a soft embrace.

Crickets sing their lullaby,
As velvety skies stretch high.
Colors fade, yet beauty stays,
In silent nightscapes, love displays.

A canvas painted deep with night,
Stars remind us: all is right.
In this peace, we find our way,
Together, beneath night's sway.

Mirrors in the Obscured

In shadows cast, reflections hide,
Truths of the heart, they coincide.
Mirrors gleam with a muted light,
Revealing dreams, lost from sight.

Faces blurred, yet souls remain,
Bound by whispers, joy, and pain.
Glimmers of hope, they fade and blend,
Each a chapter, without an end.

Through fogged glass, we seek to find,
Fragments of hearts, intertwined.
In the depths, a promise rings,
That every echo softly sings.

As time shifts like the tide of seas,
The mirrors break, yet never cease.
In the obscured, we still can see,
The beauty that's meant to be.

Traces of the Invisible

Footsteps on forgotten trails,
Whispers of winds tell ancient tales.
Moments passed, yet still they glow,
The invisible leaves traces below.

In the quiet, we sense their breath,
Echoes of life amidst the death.
Fleeting shadows, weaving through,
A dance of dreams that feels so true.

Dust of time, softly we tread,
Memories linger, never dead.
In the stillness, secrets dwell,
Traces of magic, weaved so well.

Though unseen, the bonds are strong,
In every heart, they hum a song.
Invisible threads, connecting wide,
Guide us forth, with love as our guide.

Secrets in the Twilight Mist

In whispers soft, the shadows creep,
Where secrets lie and spirits weep.
The twilight holds a gentle sigh,
As moonbeams dance in the night sky.

Through tangled trees, the pathways wind,
In corners dark, what truth we find.
A fluttering heart hears stories old,
In every leaf, a tale unfolds.

The mist conceals what daylight knows,
A symphony where silence flows.
Hidden dreams in the fading light,
Awake at last to claim the night.

With every step, the shadows blend,
To unravel secrets, time must spend.
In twilight's grip, a magic kiss,
Forever bound in the twilight mist.

Paths Winding into Mystery

Beneath the boughs where wild things grow,
The paths diverge, through dusk's soft glow.
Each step a choice, so rich, so rare,
Into the unknown, we boldly dare.

With every turn, the world expands,
In whispered tales of distant lands.
Winding deeper into the night,
A dance of shadows, lost from sight.

What treasures lie beyond the veil?
Where echoes weave their haunting tale.
In every corner, secrets wait,
An invitation to contemplate.

The winding paths to dreams ignite,
Through curves that shimmer in the light.
Into the heart of mystery,
We chase the wonders yet to be.

Clusters of Forgotten Stars

In the vast expanse of darkened skies,
Clusters of stars with ancient cries.
They flicker softly, a cosmic glow,
Whispers of stories from long ago.

Each twinkle holds a wish, a dream,
Lost in the silence, a silver stream.
Galaxies dance in the cosmic roar,
A light from ages, forevermore.

Connections fade between the night,
Yet linger on in borrowed light.
Forgotten tales on stellar shores,
In every glance, the heart explores.

These scattered jewels, in memory's hand,
Guide us gently through the starlit land.
Awake our spirits to journeys vast,
In the clusters of stars, our dreams are cast.

The Quiet Caress of Evening

As daylight fades, the colors blend,
A quiet caress, where moments mend.
Soft whispers brush against the trees,
With every sigh, a gentle breeze.

In dusk's embrace, the world finds peace,
A tender hush, where troubles cease.
The stars peek out with timid grace,
In the fading light, we find our place.

The shadows stretch like weary sighs,
As time slips on beneath soft skies.
Wrapped in warmth, the heart takes flight,
In the quiet caress of the night.

With every heartbeat, the colors fade,
A dance of moments, softly made.
In evening's arms, our spirits soar,
Through the quiet path to evermore.

Distant Lanterns in the Fog

Through the mist, they softly gleam,
Warming hearts like a forgotten dream.
Each one flickers, tales to share,
Guiding wanderers with gentle care.

Lost in shadows, whispers sing,
Hints of places, echoes cling.
A pathway veiled, but hope remains,
As distant lanterns call like trains.

In the stillness, secrets lie,
Traces of stars that once kissed the sky.
They flicker near, they dance away,
In the fog, their warmth will stay.

So follow softly, tread with grace,
Let the lanterns guide your pace.
For in their glow, the world's embraced,
In foggy nights, our dreams are traced.

Stitches in Time's Tapestry

Each thread a memory, bright or frayed,
Woven with moments, never to fade.
A patchwork piece of laughter and sighs,
Crafted in echoes, where the heart lies.

Time knows the art of careful repair,
Binding the memories, tender and rare.
In the fabric of life, we find our place,
A tapestry woven with love's embrace.

Fingers trace patterns, old stories told,
In colors vibrant, in threads of gold.
Each stitch a promise, both gentle and strong,
In the loom of existence, where we belong.

So gather your moments, let them unfold,
In the tapestry of time, let your heart hold.
For every thread tells a story sublime,
Intertwined forever, in stitches of time.

The Subtle Art of Wandering

Paths uncharted call my name,
In twilight's glow, I play the game.
With every step, the world unfolds,
In whispers soft, the mystery holds.

Curious hearts find joy in roam,
In each new place, we weave our home.
The subtle art of losing track,
In every moment, no turning back.

Beneath the sky, with stars ablaze,
I wander freely through life's maze.
Each twist and turn, an adventure waits,
In wandering souls, the magic creates.

So let me wander, wild and free,
In the heart of nature, just let me be.
For in the journey, I find my song,
The subtle art where I belong.

The Enchanted Path Ahead

Where moonlight dances on the ground,
An enchanted path awaits, profound.
With every footstep, magic flows,
In the air, the soft wind blows.

Whispers of ancient trees call low,
With secrets waiting, and tales to show.
In shadows, dreams twinkle and gleam,
Upon this path, awaken the dream.

Step lightly through the twilight glow,
Let the stars guide you where to go.
For on this road, wonders await,
Every heartbeat, a twist of fate.

So take a breath, let worries fade,
Follow the light where the dreams cascade.
In the enchanted night, find your thread,
On this magical journey, be led.

Threads of Mystery in Twilight

In the dusk where shadows creep,
Whispers dance in silence deep.
Stars awaken one by one,
Painting secrets just begun.

Beneath the shroud of evening's sigh,
Echoes ripple, dreams can fly.
A tapestry of night unfolds,
With every thread, a story told.

Moonlight weaves through ancient trees,
Carrying tales upon the breeze.
Each glimmer holds a truth within,
A journey waits where shadows spin.

Time suspends in twilight's grace,
As stars reveal their hidden face.
In quiet corners, magic swells,
Where mystery in silence dwells.

Beyond the Veil of Fog

Shrouded paths in misty gray,
Dim-lit secrets lead the way.
Footsteps soft on dampened ground,
In the fog, new worlds are found.

Figures dance just out of sight,
Fading softly with the light.
Echoes linger in the air,
While shadows weave a tale of care.

Every breath a story spun,
Beyond the veil, we drift as one.
Clarity lies where we dare,
In the fog, our spirits share.

So we wander, hearts untamed,
In the quiet, never shamed.
Through the mist, our dreams will call,
Finding truth behind the fall.

Embracing the Uncharted Path

A road unmarked, inviting chance,
Where wild flowers sway and dance.
With open hearts, we take the stride,
Into the vast, with hope our guide.

Each step forward, brave and bold,
Discoveries waiting to unfold.
The whispers of the wind are clear,
Embrace the unknown, cast off fear.

Moments fleeting, yet they last,
Lessons learned from journeys past.
In every turn, new light we find,
Illuminating paths entwined.

Together we walk, side by side,
In unison, our spirits glide.
The uncharted beckons, full of grace,
In this adventure, we find our place.

Luminescence in the Void

In the depths where silence reigns,
A spark emerges, breaking chains.
Stars ignite in cosmic dance,
Guiding souls with their romance.

Between the dark and endless night,
A glimmer fights to share its light.
Hope refracts through shadows deep,
In the void, our secrets keep.

Radiant whispers stir the calm,
With each flicker, we find a balm.
Color swirls in hues of dreams,
Luminescence softly gleams.

In vastness, we are not alone,
Through the void, our spirits roam.
For in darkness, stars align,
Creating paths where hearts entwine.